Media Madness

An Insider's Guide to Media

Fasten your seatbelts! 62 pages of media madness coming up!

Written by

Dominic Ali

Illustrated by

Michael Cho

KIDS CAN PRESS

For Noles (1939–2000) — D.A.
For Claudia, for her love and patience — M.C.

I first came across the Big Six on a Web site. A number of media educators have morphed them over the years, and they vary from teacher to teacher. Special thanks to super media ed. gurus Elizabeth Thoman at the Center for Media Literacy, Renee Hobbs and John Pungente.

'Nuff respect:
Sajida Ali
Adrian Ali
Serena Ali & Aknath Beharry
Keran & Kiana Beharry
All around hep cat Val Wyatt
Super agent Carolyn Swayze
Master illustrator Michael Cho

Props:
Danielle Adams & Tu Thanh Ha
Rick & Lori Staehling
John & Nora Vaillant
Paul Razzell & Suzanne Ahearne
Mama Kelman & Papa Fox
Bruce Grierson & Jennifer Williams
Cameron & Camellia McEwen
Prasad Bidaye
Marc Proudfoot
Toddski Custance
The gang at the David Suzuki Foundation, especially when my worlds collided ("Yo dawgs, geothermal energy is phat!")
All the media makers out there who entertain, inform and inspire

Keepin' it real:
Paul Baruzzi
J.D. Biersdorfer
The hip hop hipsters at Vancouver's The Beat 94.5 FM
CBS Evening News Sr. White House Correspondent John Roberts
Dave Catlin at Next Level Games
TV Man Sudha Krishna
Sitcom expert Peter New
Music man Panos Grames
Web dude Gerald Richardson
Much Music's Chris Nelson
Chris Taylor at Sanderson Taylor Entertainment Lawyers
The brilliant contributors to the Media-L listserv
The Vancouver Sun and indie hit factory Ogre Music for photo research
Comic king Ken Steacy
Magazine genius Lynn Cunningham

Media Madness wouldn't have been possible without the support of my Close Personal Friends (CPFs). Alas, there are too many to name. So if you're a CPF who wants to see your name in this book, print it here:

_____

Congratulations!

Text © 2005 Dominic Ali
Illustrations © 2005 Michael Cho

Kids Can Press acknowledges the financial support of the Government of Ontario, through the Ontario Media Development Corporation's Ontario Book Initiative; the Ontario Arts Council; the Canada Council for the Arts; and the Government of Canada, through the BPIDP, for our publishing activity.

Published in Canada by
Kids Can Press Ltd.
29 Birch Avenue
Toronto, ON M4V 1E2

Published in the U.S. by
Kids Can Press Ltd.
2250 Military Road
Tonawanda, NY 14150

www.kidscanpress.com

Edited by Valerie Wyatt
Designed by Julia Naimska
Printed and bound in China

The hardcover edition of this book is smyth sewn casebound.
The paperback edition of this book is limp sewn with a drawn-on cover.

CM 05 0 9 8 7 6 5 4 3 2 1
CM PA 05 0 9 8 7 6 5 4 3 2 1

National Library of Canada Cataloguing in Publication

Ali, Dominic
      Media madness : an insider's guide to media / written by Dominic Ali ; illustrated by Michael Cho.

Includes index.
ISBN 1-55337-174-7 (bound).   ISBN 1-55337-175-5 (pbk.)

1. Mass media — Juvenile literature. 2. Mass media — Influence — Juvenile literature. I. Cho, Michael II. Title.

P91.2.A45 2004   j302.23   C2004-903284-4

K_____ company

Contents

I promise it gets better on the next page.

Media Madness!

TO: Max McLoon <max@maxmcloon.com>
FROM: Dominic Ali <dom@domali.com>
SUBJECT: The Big Six to the Rescue

Welcome to *Media Madness*, Max. Freaked out by all these media? Don't be! Just ask yourself the Big Six:

1. Who created this message and why are they sending it?
2. Who is the target audience and how is the message tailored to them?
3. How does this message get your attention?
4. What values and lifestyles are shown?
5. How might other people read this message differently?
6. What's missing from this message that might be important to know?

In short, question everything!

See you later,

Dominic

WHAT'S "MEDIA" ANYWAY?

A "medium" is a method of communication. This book, for example, is a medium. If you have more than one medium, you've got "media." Media that reach a massive audience — TV, radio, video games, magazines and newspapers — are called "mass media."

We spend a lot of time with media. On average, kids aged two to seventeen spend nearly four and a half hours a day in front of electronic screens, such as televisions, computers and video games.

Four and a half hours? That's more time than I spend with my parents!

Television

I t takes a lot of smart, creative people working behind the scenes to make a successful TV show. They want their program to attract lots of advertisers who'll pay top dollar to sell products to viewers. Sure, TV entertains and informs, but it's also a business that has to make money.

Advertisers pay broadcasters for time to show their commercials. Programs are free to viewers — in exchange for watching ads.

That's where TV ratings companies come in. They track how many viewers are watching a program and use the numbers to rate the show. Large audiences mean high ratings, and high ratings mean higher prices can be charged for ad time.

TV shows live and die by ratings. If a show doesn't attract enough viewers, it's canceled to make room for one that will. Bu-bye!

Now this is more like it ... I'm a TV star! Finally the attention I so richly deserve.

Camera operator Bea Hine-Delenz shoots the action.

Makeup artist Mekya Lookgud makes the actors look great or gross, depending on the role.

Producer Hy Muckety-Muck creates the concept for the show, hires the team, oversees the co$t$ and makes the major decisions.

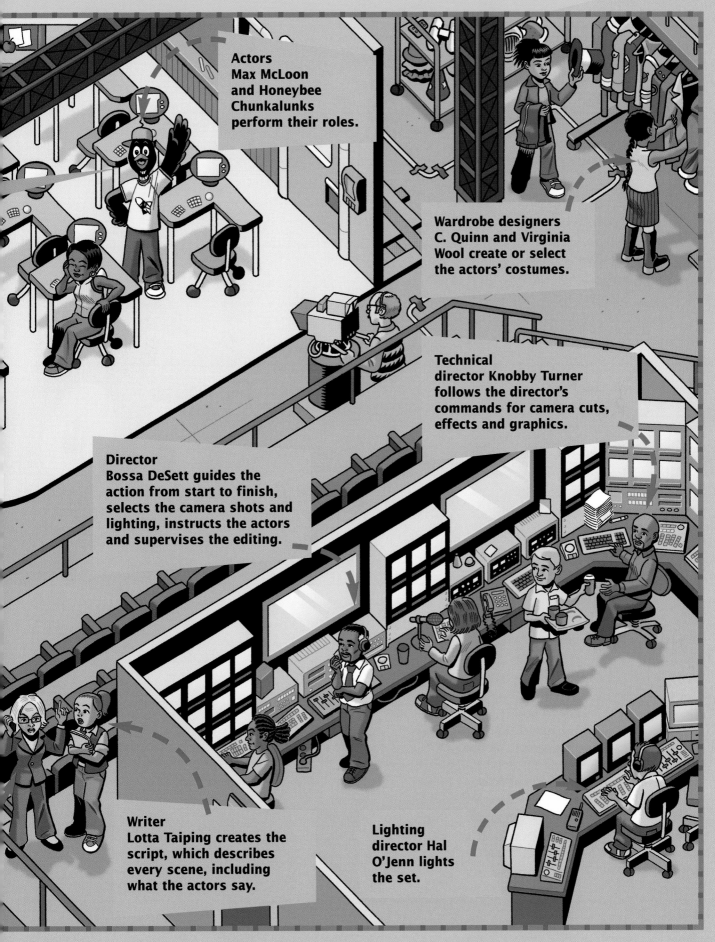

Actors
Max McLoon
and Honeybee
Chunkalunks
perform their roles.

Wardrobe designers
C. Quinn and Virginia
Wool create or select
the actors' costumes.

Technical
director Knobby Turner
follows the director's
commands for camera cuts,
effects and graphics.

Director
Bossa DeSett guides the
action from start to finish,
selects the camera shots and
lighting, instructs the actors
and supervises the editing.

Writer
Lotta Taiping creates the
script, which describes
every scene, including
what the actors say.

Lighting
director Hal
O'Jenn lights
the set.

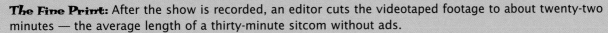
The Fine Print: After the show is recorded, an editor cuts the videotaped footage to about twenty-two minutes — the average length of a thirty-minute sitcom without ads.

Don't Believe the (Stereo)type

Max's cool new show may not be so new after all. It features characters we've all seen before on other shows. TV shows often have oversimplified characters that are "stereotypes." (In the TV biz, these stereotypes are known as "stock characters.") Some examples: the cranky neighbor, tough cop, ugly villain, beautiful princess, bratty kid and rebellious teenager.

What stereotypes about boys, girls, teenagers, senior citizens, wealthy or poor people do *you* see on TV?

Try This!

Next time you're channel surfing, play "Spot the Stereotype." Click to a show you've never seen before, watch for one minute, and see if you can find a stock character.

Some people think loons are crazy. But that's just a stereotype. Right? Right??

REALITY TV?

Most of our knowledge about the world comes through media, especially TV. But sometimes TV gives a distorted view of reality.

Researchers have found there are almost twice as many male characters as female characters on prime-time TV, even though there's an equal balance of males and females in real life. They've also found that there are very few Hispanic, Asian and Native people on prime time — far fewer than in the real world. Do the TV shows you watch represent the multicultural world you live in?

Class of 2050

Robot teachers. Virtual gym class. Hologram detention.

Welcome to School in the 21st Century!

Max McLoon
The class clown

Frank Zappatista
The quirky friend

Honeybee Chunkalunks
The cool girl

Mr. MicroChipps
The eccentric teacher

Marsha McLoon
The mischievous sister

Edison Einstein
The brain

Tiffany Saks
The snobby cheerleader

Ms. D.C. Plin
The cranky principal

Reading This Will Make You Smarter!

Come on, Max. Do you really need fake toenails? Advertisers certainly want you to think so. Companies spread the word about their products and services on TV because it reaches millions of people. But TV advertising is expensive. Each year broadcasters charge billions for ad time.

Advertisers are really interested in getting their message to kids like you. They want you to develop "brand loyalty" so you'll keep purchasing the same brand names. (Brand loyalty gets advertisers very, very excited!) You probably know someone who wears only a certain brand of jeans or sneakers. That's brand loyalty. Advertisers know that when their product gives you a good feeling, you're more likely to buy it. When you see certain products or logos, what feelings do you associate with them?

Brand loyalty??? I'd NEVER fall for that!

THE AD REVOLUTION WILL BE TELEVISED

Viewers defend themselves against ads by using remote controls and video recorders. And that scares advertisers. If you don't watch their ads, you might not buy their products. So advertisers are fighting back.

By using infomercials (long ads disguised as talk shows), virtual ads (logos digitally inserted into programs and sports events) and product placement (actual products used by actors on the TV show), advertisers hope to keep you from tuning out and turning off. And coming soon — interactive technology that will let you instantly purchase products you see on TV. If you're not careful, watching TV could become an expensive pastime.

Try This!

Imagine you're president of the Pankake Cosmetics Company and your products are aimed at young women. Which program would you advertise on?

A) *The Gnome Chompski Show:* The hilarious animated adventures of a Polish garden gnome and his zany sidekick, Ralph Nadir. This week: learn to tie shoelaces.

B) *Heaven's Doorman:* 72-year-old angel Holden Gray cries a lot and helps people get into heaven.

C) *Extreme Massive Adrenaline Rush:* Sports star Biggin Uglee shows extreme forms of entertainment. This week: cobra wrestling, human hackeysack and chainsaw Frisbee.

D) *Popular Alpha Teen:* Model Vanna Eetee interviews celebs and gossips about ex-friends. This week: makeup tips to die for.

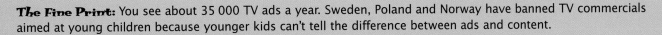

The Fine Print: You see about 35 000 TV ads a year. Sweden, Poland and Norway have banned TV commercials aimed at young children because younger kids can't tell the difference between ads and content.

Want Viewers? Jolt 'Em!

Devices such as sound effects and quick camera edits are often called "jolts" because they excite viewers and hold their attention. (And don't let Max's picture scare you. Jolts can be a lot of fun!) Some TV producers measure the success of a program by the number of jolts per minute (JPMs). Advertisements use lots of JPMs — so do music videos.

Here are some other tricks that are used to keep viewers from switching channels. Look for them next time you channel surf.

• **Theme music** at the beginning of a show sets the mood of a program. A sitcom might have bouncy music that makes you want to dance, while a crime drama might have a slow, jazzy theme. Some TV themes have even become hit songs on the radio.

• **Laugh tracks** are sounds of people laughing — from giggles to wet-your-pants guffaws — that are added to make shows sound funnier.

• **Sound effects** can make small-screen gestures more dramatic. In a fight scene you might hear a person getting hit to give the scene more ... well ... punch!

• **Background music** is often used for dramatic effect. Next time you see someone crying on a TV show, listen for the sad music.

• **Quick cuts** are a way of editing images to give them speed and motion. Compared to today's programs, older TV shows are s-l-o-w. (Some might even say g-l-a-c-i-a-l.)

A Field Guide to TV Genres

Genres are types of TV shows. Can you name a TV show for each genre below?

Genre	Description
Sitcoms	Half-hour situational comedies where the same characters appear in the same settings every week.
Dramas	Serious one-hour programs featuring fictional characters. Although they are generally aimed at adults, lots of kids like them too.
Talk shows	Programs where a host interviews real people — usually celebrities who are promoting a new film, TV show or CD.
Game shows	Real people play a game, usually for ca$h.
Tabloid shows	Copies of traditional evening newscasts that focus on entertainment news, unusual stories, gossip and celebrity scandals.
Reality TV	Real people in real life (but sometimes pretty unreal!) situations. Footage is carefully taped and edited to create a story.
Soap operas	Daily dramas about a group of characters. Each episode has an unexpected ending so viewers will tune in tomorrow.

ALL MY DUCKLINGS

Shhhh! I'm watching my favorite soap right now, so be quiet when you turn the page, okay?

The Fine Print: In the 1930s, daytime radio dramas aimed at housewives were sponsored by soap companies and were nicknamed "soap operas." The name stuck when soaps moved to TV in the 1950s.

Fighting for Eyeballs

Every day TV companies fight for your attention. By choosing to watch one show over another, you influence a show's ratings, which determine how much can be charged for advertising time. Who's fighting for *your* eyeballs?

A TV **network** is a group of stations that broadcast the same programs. Networks supply programs to local stations, called "affiliates." You probably know the

American commercial networks — ABC, CBS, Fox, NBC, UPN and WB. Canadian commercial networks include Global and CTV. Commercial networks make most of their money by charging for advertising time, so they desperately want to hold the attention of their viewers.

But not all TV is based on advertising. Many countries have **public broadcasters** that are owned or supported by taxes, businesses or individuals. In the United States, for example, the non-profit Public Broadcasting System (PBS) receives most of its funding from individual members and state governments. The Canadian Broadcasting Corporation (CBC) is funded by taxpayers, while the British Broadcasting Company (BBC) is funded by license fees from TV owners.

Public broadcasters don't rely on advertisers as much as commercial networks, so they can show controversial or critical programs that might scare off advertisers. In fact, the BBC doesn't show ads at all.

Besides the networks and public broadcasters, there are also **cable channels** that cater to specific types of viewers, such as sci-fi fans, music lovers and fashionistas. U.S. cable channels include the Discovery Channel, Nickelodeon and MTV. Canada has its own cable companies, such as the kids' station YTV and the music video channel MuchMusic.

Cable channels charge a subscription fee for their service and are so popular that they're stealing viewers from the commercial networks. To compete, the networks are making their programs a lot racier than they used to be. (That's why Max's parents send him to bed when those parental warnings appear.)

WHO'S THE BOSS?

Although there are lots of media to choose from, only about ten big companies own most of the major media you see and hear.

These media companies cross-promote their products from medium to medium, which is something they call "synergy." If you see a new TV show getting hyped by an entertainment magazine, it may be because the same company owns both the TV studio and the mag.

Many people are worried that the mass media are controlled by a handful of owners. They think this gives media owners and executives too much say in TV shows, CDs, magazines and newspapers. Imagine what would happen if the media produced TV shows aimed only at older people. We'd all be stuck watching the news and denture ads! Scary!

Watch the stereotypes there, sonny!

Your Chance to Be a TV Star!

Say you want to start a TV show about paperclip collecting, but the commercial networks, public broadcasters and cable companies aren't interested. Don't give up — there's another option. North American cable companies offer public access channels for ordinary people who want to make programs for viewers in their communities. These companies make equipment and airtime available so that anyone can make non-commercial TV. *Paperclip Roadshow*, anyone?

How to Talk TV

We've got some great talent lined up for a prime-time pilot about a high school in 2050! It'll grab our target audience during the sweeps. Syndication, here we come!

Huh?

Class of 2050

Robot teachers. Virtual gym class. Hologram detention.

Welcome to School in the 21st Century!

Relax, Max! By using the terms below, you too can sound like a genuine TV executive. Hang out in Hollywood, wear sunglasses at night, call everyone "baby"! But wait! There's more. If you read them now, we'll include a bonus definition absolutely free!

• **Talent:** This term applies to anyone who performs in front of the camera — even if they're not talented.

• **Prime time:** The time of day when most people watch TV, usually from 7 p.m. to 11 p.m. Broadcasters schedule their most popular shows at this time in order to charge the highest advertising rates. In the TV business, prime time is money. Cha-ching!

• **Pilot:** A sample episode of a new show. A successful pilot may be picked up by a network to become a regular series. Dud pilots are never heard from again.

• **Target audience:** The viewers the show is designed to appeal to. TV producers make shows to attract certain types of people that advertisers want to reach.

• **Sweeps:** At certain times during the year, ratings services measure audiences in "ratings sweepstakes." These audience numbers are used to set the ad rates that networks can charge until the next sweeps. During the sweeps, networks use sensational programming to get the highest possible ratings.

Bonus Gift!
A free definition!

• **Syndication:** TV creators sell shows to the networks, and after about four years, they may sell older episodes to individual stations. They call it syndication — you call it reruns.

Are You Watching Too Much TV?

If you answer "yes" to three or more questions below, maybe you should turn off the TV. (If you can make it off the couch, that is!)

Do you talk only in TV catchphrases?

Is your thumb the strongest part of your body?

Do you refuse to go camping because you can't change the channel on the campfire?

Do you check the weather channel instead of opening the window to see if it's raining?

Can you sing the theme song to every sitcom ever made, but can't remember the lyrics to the national anthem?

The Scoop on TV News

LOON NEWS AT NOON

UBC

Here at Loon News, I don't make the news ... I just distort it.

Speak for yourself, Max! TV reporters work hard to bring the day's events to their viewers as accurately as possible. And they have an important job. TV news is powerful. Most people find out about the goings-on in the world and their communities from TV news, and newscasts can influence the way viewers think and feel about current issues and people.

Newscasts consist of stories, which might include videotaped interviews, visuals or on-the-scene reports that are edited to follow the reporter's voice-over. Stories may also be read by the news anchor, with or without visuals.

Although newscasts are about actual events instead of fictional ones, they still have to attract viewers and appeal to advertisers. Like sitcoms and dramas, newscasts have tricks to keep viewers watching. Here's how they do it:

• **Action footage** makes events seem dramatic and super important.

• **Attractive news anchors** are easy on the eyes.

• **Gruesome events,** such as crimes, disasters and wars, grab your attention.

• **A funny story** at the end of the newscast finishes the program on a happy note.

What other tricks do newscasts use to keep viewers glued to the set?

How to Get on the Six O'Clock News

You don't have to commit a crime or be famous to get on the news. It's much easier than that. Companies and politicians often organize press conferences — invitation-only events where journalists can ask questions and videotape newsmakers.

Companies may also produce video news releases (VNRs), which are pre-recorded videotapes containing interviews, exciting visuals and info about their latest accomplishments. VNRs make it easy for reporters to construct a news story. Maybe too easy. Some news organizations may occasionally run VNRs without additional reporting, so viewers end up with only one side of a story — the company's side.

TV AROUND THE WORLD

In 1999, over 98 percent of North American households had TV sets. The world average was just 23 percent.

Wow! If they don't have TV sets, who does the babysitting?

Journalism Jargon

Want to sound like a seasoned TV journalist? Here's your chance!

• **Anchor:** An on-screen journalist who reads the news and introduces reports from correspondents.

• **Photo-op:** A staged "photo opportunity" where the press is encouraged to videotape a newsmaker. Some people will go to great lengths for a memorable photo-op — one politician even staged a news conference where he showed up on a Jet Ski.

• **Stand-up:** A reporter videotaped standing in front of a news conference or event.

• **Live shot:** An unedited segment that is broadcast to viewers while the event is occurring, without editing. (Most news stories are recorded and edited, then broadcast later.) Because live shots give viewers a sense that they're at the scene, newscasts often include them — even though nothing much may be happening.

• **Sound bite:** A brief portion of a speech or interview, usually lasting only a few seconds, that contains a memorable quote.

• **Reaction shot:** A shot showing a reporter responding to the interviewee with a nod or a smile. These are usually filmed separately from the interview and edited into the final video.

• **Tease:** A voice-over or visual that gets viewers excited about an upcoming story so they won't switch channels.

• **Crawl:** Usually seen on news-only channels, this is text that scrolls by at the bottom of the screen.

Makin' Music

Rock on! The Max McLoon Experience is in the studio, recording songs for its first CD. The CD will be one of approximately 27 000 new releases that hit the market each year. Record companies around the world ship millions of CDs to retail stores and make billions of dollars in sales. (No word on how many CDs feature an accordion-playing loon, though!)

Max and his bandmates aren't the only ones who hope their CD will become a best-selling smash. Record companies need hit songs. The average record label loses money on about 90 percent of the records it releases, relying on a few megahits to make money.

Producer
Juana Gold-Reckid supervises all aspects of the recording.

Manager
Ed Vice looks after the band's business and creative decisions.

A&R
(artist & repertoire) scout
Les Maykadeal works for a record company, finding cool new talent and hot new songs.

TO: Max McLoon <max@maxmcloon.com>

FROM: Dominic Ali <dom@domali.com>

SUBJECT: Musician Jokes

Hey, Max, thought you'd like these! — Dominic

Q: How many singers does it take to screw in a lightbulb?
A: One. The world revolves around her.

Q: Why did the band fire its guitar player?
A: He kept stringing them along.

Q: What do you call a dependable drummer who shows up when he's supposed to, always plays in time to the music and never complains?
A: A computer.

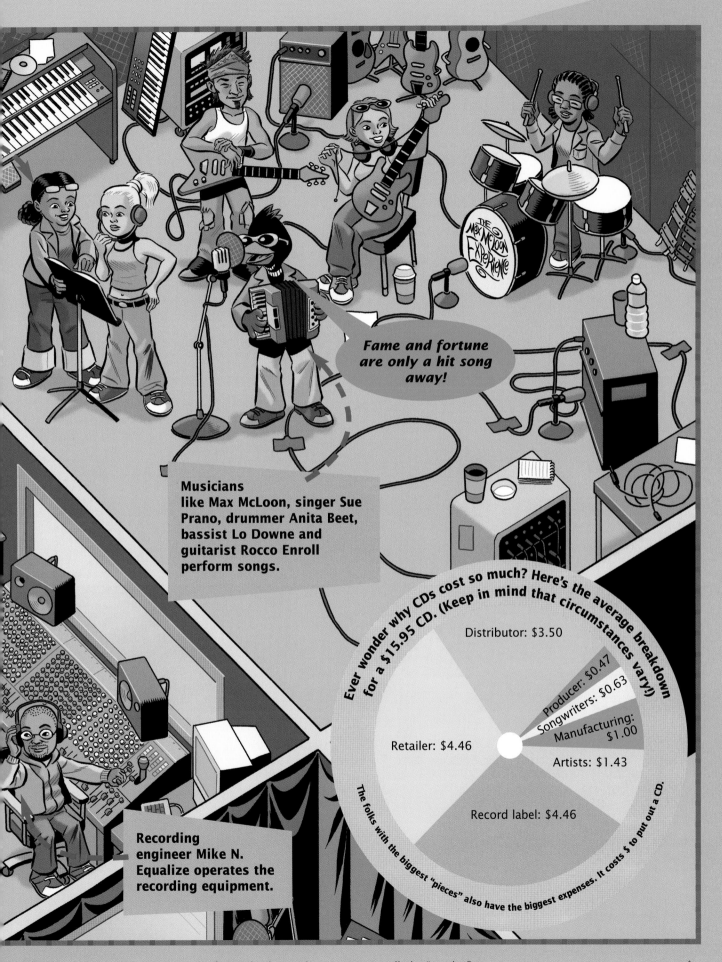

Fame and fortune are only a hit song away!

Musicians like Max McLoon, singer Sue Prano, drummer Anita Beet, bassist Lo Downe and guitarist Rocco Enroll perform songs.

Recording engineer Mike N. Equalize operates the recording equipment.

Ever wonder why CDs cost so much? Here's the average breakdown for a $15.95 CD. (Keep in mind that circumstances vary!)

Distributor: $3.50

Producer: $0.47

Songwriters: $0.63

Manufacturing: $1.00

Artists: $1.43

Retailer: $4.46

Record label: $4.46

The folks with the biggest "pieces" also have the biggest expenses. It costs $ to put out a CD.

The Fine Print: The percentage of record sales paid to an artist is called a "royalty."

Watching Music

Would you watch a TV channel with nothing but commercials? Guess what? You already do. Music videos are actually big flashy commercials provided by record companies to music video channels. They hope the videos will encourage you to buy CDs.

When videos first became popular in the 1980s, many performers felt they robbed fans of using their imaginations when listening to music. But other artists such as Madonna and Michael Jackson creatively used videos as an art form. Their records flew off the shelves. Now videos are an important way to boost record sales.

Performers use videos to craft their images so they'll have maximum appeal to their target audience. If Max wanted to appeal to hip-hop fans, his video might show him break-dancing, wearing fancy clothes or cruising around in a cool car. Sometimes the image in the music video is just an image, with very little connection to reality.

Apply the Big Six (see page 5) to your favorite videos. You might be surprised at what you discover.

Talk about image! It's hard to believe we're the same band.

YOU WANT MUSIC VIDEOS ... THEY WANT EYEBALLS!

Music video channels play a small list of regular videos called a "playlist." The most popular videos are put in "heavy rotation" — they're played more often than videos in medium or light rotation. Each week, new videos may be added to the playlist, bumping off older, less popular ones.

Music videos use lots of tricks to keep you glued to the set, such as quick-cut edits, exciting visuals, special effects and great-looking people dressed in cool clothes. Some videos also feature dialogue, like in a movie, that turns the song into a story. What other tricks do videos and music channels use to keep you watching? Does it work?

Like all commercial TV, music video channels want to attract viewers they can turn around and sell to advertisers. Advertisers want to reach young people with money to spend. They know that the tastes you develop when you're young stay with you for a long time.

Try This!

If you have the technology, enlist some friends as actors and make a new video of your favorite song. Can't get your hands on a video camera? No problem. Create a storyboard with drawings that show the action you'd like to see in your video.

23

CD Cover Lover

CD covers are an amazing art form. Some classic covers are the Beatles' *Sgt. Pepper's Lonely Hearts Club Band* and *Abbey Road*, Pink Floyd's *Dark Side of the Moon* and Madonna's *Like a Virgin*. (Aside from the covers, the music on these CDs is pretty cool, too!)

Like cereal boxes and candy wrappers, CD covers are also designed to sell a product. They help performers shape their image and attract a specific audience. Try applying the Big Six (see page 5) to Max's CD covers. What types of music fans would buy these CDs?

Try This!

A local hard-rock group wants you to design their next CD cover. Will you use a photograph or an illustration? Will you use an easy-to-read type or a CRAZY one? How will the group look? Tattoos and shaved heads or nice suits and short hair? (You might choose not to include the group on the cover at all.) Once you've designed the CD, create a poster for the band's upcoming concert tour.

Decision, decisions ... Which image works best for my music?

Turn On and Tune In the Radio

If you think radio DJs can play whatever they want, think again. They have to stick to the playlist — the list of songs drawn up by the music director.

The music director decides on the playlist by consulting national music charts that appear in industry magazines such as *Billboard*. She also researches listeners' requests and meets with record companies to find out what's new. The playlist is carefully tailored to appeal to the station's target audience.

The goal of a commercial radio station like LOON Radio is to attract a large and loyal audience so it can sell advertising time. As with TV, ratings services measure the popularity of radio stations. The larger the audience, the higher the ratings, the more the station can charge advertisers.

Money from advertisers keeps the radio station in business so it can employ friendly DJs to introduce music and keep listeners tuned in.

DIRECTIONS FOR GREAT RADIO — MIX AND REPEAT

Ever notice how a song you don't like at first becomes catchier the more you hear it? Well, people in the music biz know that too. The more you hear a song, the greater the chances you'll come to like it enough to buy the CD. One of the keys to success in the music biz is repeat, repeat, repeat. That's why radio airplay is important for record companies.

So how do new CDs get on the air? It's not easy. Even well-known performers may have trouble getting their latest songs added to playlists. It's even harder for first-time bands nobody has ever heard. That's why major record labels send radio stations free CDs and meet with music directors to persuade them to add new songs to the playlist.

Try This!

Unleash your inner DJ! Get together with your friends and create a radio show using audio editing software or a cassette tape recorder. Don't forget to record yourself introducing the songs so listeners will know what they're hearing.

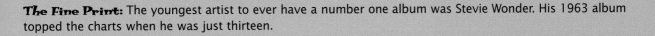

The Fine Print: The youngest artist to ever have a number one album was Stevie Wonder. His 1963 album topped the charts when he was just thirteen.

Playin' That Funky Music

ach radio station has its own "format" — content and style designed to reach an audience of a specific age, background and income.

Although there are dozens of formats to choose from, here are some of the most common ones. Do you have stations like these in your town?

Format	What you can expect	Max's analysis
Top 40	The forty most popular hits from the national music charts, aimed at people aged fifteen to thirty.	"All these songs are about love. But that's okay. They've all got a good beat you can dance to."
Urban Contemporary	R&B, hip-hop and sometimes house and dance music that's popular with young urban listeners.	"These phat trax make me wanna shake my booty and use bad spelling."
Alternative	Cutting-edge alternative rock and songs from the past year.	"This music hasn't sold out and gone commercial ... yet."
Classic Rock	Old rock & roll hits from the 1960s to the 1990s and a few modern hits for listeners aged thirty to fifty.	"These tunes always remind my grandparents of the time they danced naked in the mud at Woodstock."
Easy Listening	Soft rock and ballads from the past forty years for listeners over thirty-five.	"Feeling ... very ... drowsy ... eyelids ... getting ... heavier ... zzzzz."

BREAK ON THROUGH TO THE OTHER SIDE

When a performer best known for one musical style has a recording that becomes popular in another musical category, it's called a "crossover." A rapper, for example, might record a song with a rock group in order to have her latest single played on rock stations. Performers can sell more records if they have a crossover hit. It remains to be seen if there's room on the pop charts for Max's unique blend of polka–reggae–hip–hop–metal!

The Fine Print: One way record companies promote new artists is to have them appear as featured guests on songs with established performers.

Making Radio Magic

One of the best ways to draw customers to a new product is to give them a free sample. That's what makes radio so important. It gives listeners free samples of new songs.

But in order to deliver these free samples, radio stations must first attract listeners. Apply the Big Six (see page 5) to your favorite radio station. See if it uses any of these clever tricks to keep you tuned in:

• **Enthusiastic DJs** with funny personalities and crazy on-air voices tell lots of jokes or stir up controversy. Morning teams ("zoo crews") and rush hour DJs are on at peak times to attract listeners in their cars.

• **Countdowns** keep listeners coming back to hear if their favorite songs are going up or down on the charts and to find out what's number one.

• **Phone-ins and requests** give listeners the chance to get on the air and feel famous — if only for a few seconds.

• **Contests:** If you are the first reader to guess that DJs run contests to keep listeners tuned in, you're a smart cookie!

Radio is like ear candy ... and the first hit is always free!

HUNTING FOR FRESH TRACKS

Tired of the same music on the radio? Well, you're in luck! Try tuning into community stations or student-run college radio stations. They usually don't have playlists, so DJs can play anything they want. That means you'll hear music you might not hear anywhere else. Also check out Internet-only radio stations. Stations in other countries often broadcast music online so you can discover what their popular songs are.

Back in the U.S.S.R. ...

Selling Sounds

Pssst! Wanna buy a CD?

Recording a CD is hard work, but selling one — or several million — is even harder. Here are some ways musicians promote their CDs:

- Going on concert tours across the country.
- Giving interviews to TV stations, radio, newspapers and magazines.
- Appearing at record stores to sign CDs and meet fans.
- Getting their songs included on movie soundtracks or compilation CDs, which feature music by different artists.
- Creating official Web sites, which may feature news, online diaries, biographies, upcoming concert dates or downloadable photos.
- Sending their CDs to music critics who, they hope, will give a thumbs-up review. (That's why music reviewers always have the biggest CD collections!)

Shh! Music Secret!

One thing radio station music directors look for in a new song is a "hook" — a catchy musical phrase that will grab listeners in the first thirty seconds. Hooks are usually repeated throughout the song. Can you pick out the hooks in your favorite songs? (Hint: They're usually the parts of the songs that you find yourself humming.)

SODA POP MUSIC?

TV advertisers sometimes pay to use a popular song in a commercial. They hope that listeners who like the song will transfer their feelings to the product. Having a song in a commercial can have another payback — it can boost CD sales.

Although commercials may give a song lots of exposure, some people think the meaning changes when a song is used to sell a product. Does the meaning of a love song change if it's used to sell soda pop?

Future Music

Wanna scare a record company executive? Tell him you never buy music CDs because you're too busy trading music files with your friends and burning your own.

Computers make it easy for music fans to convert CDs into digital sound files that can be sent over the Internet. Sounds great, right? But when you download music without paying for it, the musicians don't get paid royalties. (See page 21.)

Record companies have tried to shut down online music services that allow music fans to swap songs. As far as they're concerned, downloading music without paying for it is stealing. To stop this, they have experimented with copy protection that makes it difficult to convert tracks to digital sound files. They've also created their own online music services where listeners can download music for a small fee.

But downloading music for free has its defenders. Some unknown bands want listeners to hear their music even if they don't earn any royalties. And some fans want to sample the merchandise before shelling out for a CD. No one is really sure how we'll be listening to and buying music in the future. So stay tuned!

Magazines

There's a little more to magazines than glamorous parties and clothes, Max. Creative teams put in long hours to produce magazines we'll want to read. Mags are all about circulation — the number of copies of each issue that are distributed. In general, the bigger the circulation, the more a magazine can charge for advertising.

There are two main ways of getting mags into the hands and eyes of readers — subscriptions and newsstand sales. (There are also controlled circulation mags that are sent at no cost to people in certain occupations.)

Very few mags support themselves on subscriptions and newsstand sales. Most make money by selling advertising space. Money from advertisers helps the magazine pay the photographers and writers who provide the editorial content.

Magazines attract certain types of readers by reflecting a lifestyle or attitude that appeals to their target audiences. This helps advertisers pitch their products to those most likely to buy. For example, which magazine would you advertise Max's CD in: *Accordion Music Monthly,* aimed at accordion-loving music fans, or *Turn That Noise Off!*, the mag for people who hate music?

Shh! Magazine Secret!

Ever wonder what happens to unsold magazines when new issues hit the newsstands? Sometimes the old mags are returned to the publisher, but more often, just the covers are returned. The rest of the mag goes into the shredder.

Cool parties. Celebs. Great clothes. This is the life!

Editor-in-chief Max McLoon is in charge of the magazine's editorial (non-advertising) content.

Art director Hal Vetica commissions photographers and illustrators, oversees photo shoots and designs the magazine pages.

The Fine Print: Larger magazines also employ fact-checkers who verify the facts in each article and screen to avoid for potential lawsuits.

Publisher
Mayka Z. Bucks is in charge of the magazine's business dealings and leads the ad sales team.

Writer
Wordy Smith, photographer Otto Focuss and illustrator Walter Kolor create the words, photos and art for the magazine.

Editor
Hackett Tubitz plans stories, hires writers and oversees articles to make sure they're accurate and interesting.

Copy editor Emmanuelle O'Style checks the articles for spelling and grammar.

Advertising salesperson Di L. Tone meets with potential advertisers to sell space in the magazine.

Production manager Manny Details prepares the mag for the printer.

Glossy Mags, Glossier Ads

Ever notice how magazine ads like the one below try to sell you on the ideal life? Their message: If you buy our product, you'll be cooler, smarter, prettier and more popular. Many ads show a product saving a consumer from an embarrassing situation. Others show flattering photos of models and celebrities using the product. In kids' magazines, ads are often designed to look like puzzles, contests and crafts.

Some ads don't even appear to sell products. For example, an ad for running shoes might show an empty basketball court, with no sneakers in sight. Instead of showing the products, they encourage readers to associate good feelings with their brand name.

Think of a brand, such as a clothing store or fast-food restaurant. What good or bad qualities do you associate with it? Why?

WASTE - ⊙ -DOUGH®

Cool beak rings for cool loons.™

AVAILABLE WHEREVER
FINE BEAK RINGS
ARE SOLD.

The Fine Print: Researchers estimate that youth between eight and nineteen will spend more than $240 billion in 2007. That's why advertisers love you!

TO: Max McLoon <max@maxmcloon.com>
FROM: Dominic Ali <dom@domali.com>
SUBJECT: Putting the Big Six into Action

Hey, Max,
It's easy and fun to apply the Big Six (see page 5) to magazine ads! Here's my take on the ad on page 36:

>1. Who created this message and why are they sending it?
Waste-O-Dough® created this ad to sell loons its newest beak ring.

>2. Who is the target audience and how is the message tailored to them?
Loons around age seventeen or eighteen, because they're the ones most likely to buy beak rings. The message is tailored to them because it shows good-looking models who are the same age as the target audience.

>3. How does this message get your attention?
This ad uses Max's familiar face and beautiful loonettes to attract attention.

>4. What values and lifestyles are shown?
Loons who wear beak rings are cool and popular.

>5. How might other people read this message differently?
Some people think beak rings are a total waste of $.

>6. What's missing from this message that might be important to know?
That beak rings are made out of cheap plastic and break easily!

Now it's your turn. Good Luck!
Dominic

Try This!

Give magazines a swift kick in the ads! It's easy to see what's in a magazine ad, but it's harder to see what's missing. (Most ads don't mention a product's negative side.) Your mission, should you choose to accept it, is to write an honest ad. Rip out a magazine ad and rewrite it to tell the full story.

GROAN!
Where's the bathroom? I'm gonna be SICK!

STEALTH ADS

Advertorials are long ads designed to look and read like genuine magazine stories. But don't be fooled. These sneaky ads are written and paid for by advertisers. Careful readers will spot the fine print: This is an advertising supplement. **They may also notice that** the advertorial is printed in a different typeface than the rest of the mag.

Shh! Mag Secret!

Magazines use media kits to reach potential advertisers. Kits usually include age and income info about the magazine's readers, advertising rates and a free issue. (Some mags even post these media kits online.) Write to your favorite magazine for a media kit and see how they attract advertisers.

Photos + Stories = Magazine Success

Photos are an important part of magazines. In fact, some readers pick up certain magazines just for the pictures. But beware ... photos aren't always what they appear to be.

Computer programs make it easy for art directors and photographers to alter photos. They can improve a photo, say, by removing a distracting sign behind someone's head.

Photos of magazine models can also be changed to remove freckles and birthmarks, smooth wrinkles and whiten teeth. Hair color can be changed and effects added. Truth is, models don't look nearly as good in real life as they do in magazines. But that doesn't stop lots of people from trying to look like them.

Magazine art directors aren't trying to trick readers — they just want photos to look as good as possible. But mistakes do happen. A New York fashion magazine once published a pic of a supermodel missing her bellybutton!

Forget exercise — all you need is computer software to get the body of a magazine model!

It's a shame I can't use software to remove distracting things from my real life — like homework.

KNOW YOUR MAGAZINES

Next time you visit a newsstand, see if you can find examples of these common magazine types.

■ **Consumer magazines** are sold on newsstands and by subscription. These mags contain advertising and are meant for the general public.

■ **Trade magazines** are intended for people in specific occupations. There are mags for almost every job, including farmers, bakers, hairstylists, actors and truckers.

■ **Magalogs,** a combination of magazine and catalog, are produced by companies to sell their products or enhance their image. Magalogs don't usually contain any critical articles.

The Stories

In addition to photos, magazines need stories that will grab the attention of their readers. For many mags, stories about celebrities are the biggest draw. There's nothing like a supermodel or a rock star to move a magazine.

It's the editor-in-chief's job to make sure the mix of stories in each issue fits the "personality" of the mag. After all, mags have to deliver readers to advertisers.

Ideas for stories are usually developed by the magazine's editors and writers. Some may be borrowed from other media, such as newspapers or TV, then further researched and written specially for the magazine.

Ideas also come from companies that want mags to mention their products. For example, travel companies often invite editors on free trips, and entertainment companies send free books, CDs and movie passes in the hope of getting positive reviews.

You mean I have to write something in exchange for all these free goodies? There's always a catch ...

Keepin' You Readin'!

Just as TV shows use lots of JPMs to keep you glued to the set (see page 12), and radio DJs keep you listening to their stations, magazines use eye-popping visuals and snappy stories to keep you coming back. The longer you spend with a magazine, the more likely you are to subscribe — and purchase products that are advertised in it. Here are some other attention-grabbing techniques to look for the next time you're flipping through your fave mag:

• **Factoids:** Weird and wonderful snippets of information. "It's a fact! In 2002, more than 17 000 magazines were available in the U.S.!"

• **Sidebars:** Mini-articles attached to a main story.

• **Q & A:** Articles where the writer's questions (Q) and the subject's answers (A) both appear, making you feel you were there when the interview took place.

• **Features:** Longer articles designed to interest the mag's target audience.

• **Photo spreads:** A series of photographs spread across several pages. Most of the time they show models wearing the latest trendy clothes.

• **Games and quizzes:** Do you think a series of short questions meant to be answered by a magazine's readers are:
a) a neat way to make readers feel involved in a magazine?
b) fun?
c) a good way to break up the stories and photo spreads?
d) all of the above?
If you answered "d," you are a magazine genius!

Some magazines use other tricks to keep readers interested, like centerfolds, trading cards, comic strips and posters. How do your favorite magazines keep you hooked?

'ZINE FIENDS!

Thousands of people around the world publish their own 'zines — small-circulation magazines. 'Zines can be about anything and may include interviews, journal entries, drawings or photographs. You can find 'zines in some record and comic book shops. Check 'em out — you may want to start your own.

Try This!

Become a magazine archaeologist! If you want to see the strange customs and unusual clothing of ancient societies, flip through some old magazines. Check out the ads, especially for clothes and cars. Hard to believe those styles were once considered cool, isn't it? Will your favorite magazines look this funny in the future?

Comic Books

Crash! Bang! Boom! Although you can speed through a comic book in a few minutes, it takes a talented team of artists and writers hours to create one.

Publishers of comic books make money from selling comics and advertising. As with other forms of media, the bigger the audience, the more publishers can charge for ad space.

Here are some ways comic book publishers keep readers coming back month after month:

- A "hook" on the opening splash page — usually an action scene — captures your interest immediately.
- Complicated storylines are always "to be continued," so readers must buy the next issue to find out what happens.
- Popular characters from one comic may "star" in their own separate title so that fans will be tempted to buy the new book as well as the regular one.

Pretty smart, eh?! Next time you're flipping through a comic book, see if you can find other ways publishers keep readers hooked.

Shh! Comics Secret!

In 1954, Dr. Fredric Wertham published *Seduction of the Innocent,* which claimed comics turned children into criminals. This led to the creation of the Comics Code Authority (CCA) — a rating assuring parents that a comic was appropriate for kids. You can still see the CCA stamp of approval on some comics today.

Editor Rhea Vise supervises the team.

Colorist Roy G. Biv scans the art into a computer and adds color.

Letterer Arial Phont arranges the words (dialogue, sound effects and narration) on the page.

The Fine Print: Nowadays, the people who work on a comic book may not be in the same office, or even the same city! Thanks to the Internet, fax and phone, they can work together long distance.

Comic Conundrum

Comic books are loaded with amazing characters, from caped crusaders to spooky monsters and cute animals. Because there are so many exotic and unusual characters, it's sometimes hard to tell who's *missing* in comic books.

Although the real world is full of men and women in equal job positions, you might not guess that from reading most comic books. Men are usually in the lead roles, while women take second place. And although there are some black, Asian, Hispanic and Native comic heroes, most are white. Characters who aren't white are often in supporting roles or appear as guest stars.

You may also notice that female superheroes are dressed in tighter-fitting and more revealing costumes than male characters. Check out the body types in comics, too. Most male characters have sculpted bodies while females are usually slim and well-endowed. Do you need the body of a weightlifter or a swimsuit model to be a superhero?

However, there are signs that things are changing. Comics nowadays have more culturally and physically diverse characters than they used to. And they can still kick the butts of evil-doers and leap tall buildings in a single bound.

(UN)SUPER-HEROES?

Not all comics are about superheroes. Some comic book pros write and illustrate books based on their lives or those of other real people. There are also comics based on the great heroes of literature. One company turned classic books like *Moby Dick* and William Shakespeare's *Hamlet* into comics. If it weren't for those illustrated classics, countless people would've flunked high school English!

Hey! Who's missing?

I have a super power — I can mess up my room faster than a tornado!

Try This!

Is there a super-talented comic book artist lurking beneath your mild-mannered exterior? Grab a pencil and some paper and go for it!

Draw some panels on a blank sheet, then add some speech and thought bubbles and sound effects.

If you're really inspired, break out your pencil crayons and color your comics. Then run off copies on a color photocopier and trade your comic with friends. (Lots of professional comic book artists started out this way.)

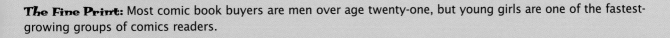

The Fine Print: Most comic book buyers are men over age twenty-one, but young girls are one of the fastest-growing groups of comics readers.

Today Comics, Tomorrow the World!

If you play with an action figure or wear a t-shirt featuring your favorite comic character, you're seeing licensing in action.

Characters like Max McLoon are called "properties" in the multimillion-dollar licensing biz. In exchange for money, the owners of these properties give permission to companies who want to use the characters on toys or clothes. So if a toy company wanted permission to create a Max McLoon action figure, they'd have to pay a fee to the person who created him. (Nudge, nudge, wink, wink!)

Companies like to license popular properties because they know they have a following. Some movies, for example, are based on popular comic characters. Publishers hope fans of the comic book will also go to the movie.

SILVER SCREEN SUPERHEROES

Here are some big screen movies based on comics:

- Hellboy (released 2004)
- Hulk (2003)
- Daredevil (2003)
- Spider-Man (2002)
- X-Men (2000)
- Blade (1998)
- Spawn (1997)
- Men in Black (1997)
- Judge Dredd (1995)
- Casper (1995)
- The Mask (1994)
- Richie Rich (1994)
- Teenage Mutant Ninja Turtles (1990)
- Batman (1989)
- Annie (1982)
- Superman (1978)

WORLD-O-COMICS

Comics are an international medium.

- In Japan, comics — called manga — account for 40 percent of all printed material sold. They're also growing in popularity in North America.
- France's *Asterix* comics have been translated into forty languages and have sold more than 220 million books worldwide.
- In 1929, Belgian artist Georges Remi — better known as Hergé — created one of the world's best-known comic characters, boy reporter Tintin.

Try This!

The Moola-Moola Comic Book Company wants you to design a character it can license to other companies. What special qualities will your character possess? Which companies would you allow to use your character? Are there any companies you wouldn't want using your creation?

The Fine Print: It's not just comic books that play the licensing game. Fashion designers also license their names to products they haven't personally created, such as perfume and bed linen.

Newspapers

I t takes a lot of smart people to assemble a newspaper each day. Newspaper reporters cover news events and interview the people involved. Photographers snap the pics to go with the stories. Editors decide which stories to include in the newspaper and make sure the articles are easy to understand. Then the printing presses roll, and the delivery people get the papers to newsstands and subscribers. And the next day they do it all over again!

Like other forms of mass media, newspapers survive by selling copies to readers and space to advertisers. (Many cities also have free weekly newspapers financed entirely by ads.)

Papers attract readers by providing information about news, entertainment and sports events. They also have classifieds sections, advice columns, horoscopes, crossword puzzles and comics. (Just think of them as Web sites printed on big sheets of paper that are updated daily.)

Try This!

Give yourself a birthday present! Visit your local library and read the newspaper from the day you were born. Did any major events take place? (If you need help finding the newspaper, ask a librarian.)

Photographer Meg Hapixel takes the photos that accompany articles.

Photo editor Claire Optix supervises the photographers and advises the editors on the best photos for the articles.

Editor Earl E. Dedlyne supervises all aspects of the newspaper's editorial content.

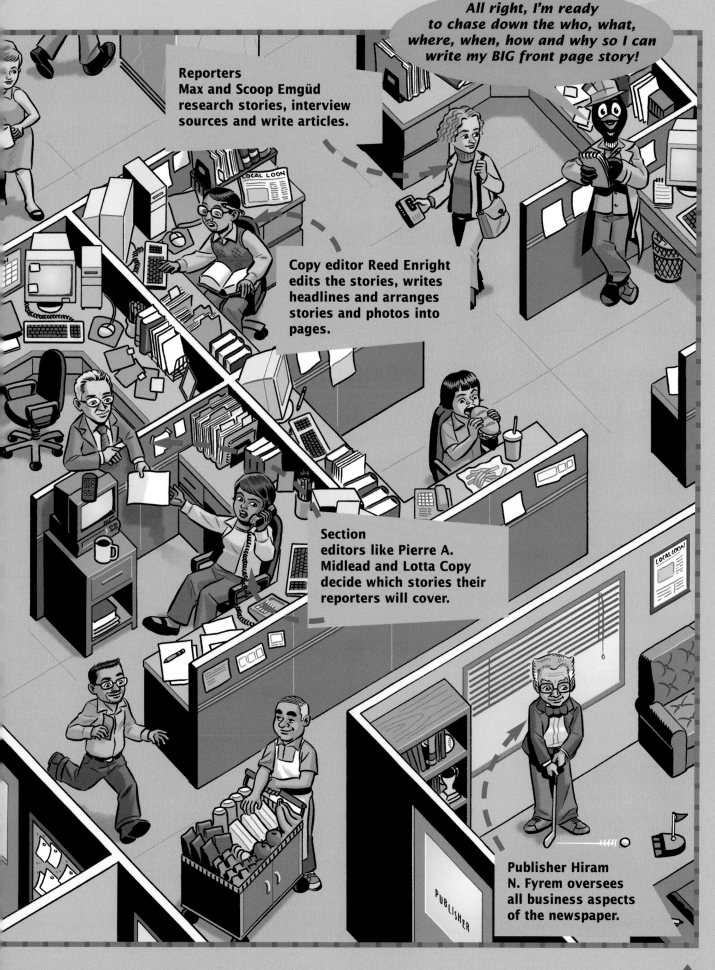

All right, I'm ready to chase down the who, what, where, when, how and why so I can write my BIG front page story!

Reporters Max and Scoop Emgüd research stories, interview sources and write articles.

Copy editor Reed Enright edits the stories, writes headlines and arranges stories and photos into pages.

Section editors like Pierre A. Midlead and Lotta Copy decide which stories their reporters will cover.

Publisher Hiram N. Fyrem oversees all business aspects of the newspaper.

Whose News?

Egg's fall prompts expensive rescue attempt

Yesterday, Humpty Dumpty sat on a wall and fell off. The King's horses and men were summoned but arrived too late to save the egg.

The King, who is on a nine-week Caribbean cruise vacation, commented, "Calling all those horses and men costs money. He shouldn't have been on the wall in the first place." He warned that he would not tolerate a repeat of Humpty Dumpty's stunt.

Tragic fall raises safety concerns

Yesterday, Humpty Dumpty sat on a wall and fell off. Although the King's horses and men tried to rescue Mr. Dumpty, he could not be saved.

The King, speaking to reporters while on vacation, expressed sympathy to Mr. Dumpty's family. "He shouldn't have been on the wall in the first place," he said, clearly distressed. The King expressed his hope that, in future, tragic deaths like this wouldn't happen again.

Newspapers are full of facts (reports of things that actually happened) and opinions (beliefs open to debate). Fact: Max is a loon. Opinion: Max is a loony loon.

Newspapers try to make it clear which is which. Opinions appear in columns — short articles written by regular columnists — and on the editorial pages.

"Soft news" (feature stories) about trends, personalities and lifestyles may also include writers' opinions. "Hard news" stories about specific events such as crimes or accidents are supposed to provide facts without opinions. However, sometimes opinions do creep in. Reporters are people, too, and they have their own beliefs and life experiences. They may not even be aware that they are biased (favor one side over another).

Occasionally, bias is not accidental. Reporters may feel pressure to write a story a certain way or avoid a story altogether. Why? Newspaper owners may send subtle messages that certain stories are off-limits. Or advertisers may threaten to yank their ads over unflattering coverage. Or prominent people may threaten to sue if they feel they've been unfairly treated in an article. All these factors may result in biased stories.

Try applying the Big Six (see page 5) to the stories on the left. Can you spot the bias in them?

WHAT'S NEWS, PUSSYCAT?

Each day journalists and editors must decide which events are newsworthy enough to make it into the paper. Here's what they look for:

☑ **The story is occurring now or soon or is connected to a current event or issue.**
☑ **The story has never been covered before or is a new way of looking at an old issue.**
☑ **The information in the story is useful to readers.**

SUPPLEMENTS EXPOSED

From time to time newspapers publish special sections, sometimes called "supplements." Although these special sections look like the rest of the newspaper, they're actually advertising in disguise. In a Flossing Awareness Month special section, for example, you might find ads for White Paint™ toothpaste and floss, an article about how much people love flossing and an advertorial about a great dentist in town — written by the dentist!

Try This!

Put your newspaper on an advertising diet! Take the news or arts section of your local newspaper and cut out all of the ads. How much is left?

News-speak

our editor isn't threatening you, Max! If you want to work for a newspaper, you'd better learn the lingo:

• **Scoop:** Publishing an important story before other newspapers.

• **Beat:** A subject area of the newspaper — sports, business, crime — that a reporter regularly writes about.

• **Wires:** International and national services that electronically distribute news and photos to papers around the world.

• **Angle:** A writer's approach to an article. Two writers may write about toys, for example, but one might focus on toy safety while the other might focus on a toy manufacturer.

• **Lead:** An article's first few sentences, which tell readers the who, what, where, when, why and how of the story. (Often spelled "lede.")

• **Morgue:** The newspaper library where published articles, photos and resources are kept for reference.

The Fine Print: Now that information is stored electronically for reporters to access, the term "morgue" is disappearing.

Worth a Thousand Words

Just as newspapers depend on reporters to write great stories, they rely on photographers to snap interesting pictures. Photos are important. Years after an event has taken place, readers may remember only a few facts. But a picture can be fixed in their minds forever.

Good newspaper photos tell a story, add information to written articles and show action as it happens. Photographers also want their pictures to show a particular viewpoint about the event they're capturing and trigger an emotional response from readers.

Newspaper photographers aren't allowed to use computer software to make major changes to their photos. But minor changes — like adjusting the lighting or cropping (see sidebar) — are acceptable. (If a photo is drastically altered, it's usually labeled so readers aren't confused into thinking what they're seeing actually happened.)

Don't forget to apply the Big Six (see page 5) to the photos you see in your newspaper. You might be surprised at what you discover.

The best thing about being a photographer? Wearing a cool vest with a million pockets!

CROPPING

Photos are usually "cropped" — some parts are trimmed off — to maximize impact, eliminate distracting details and save space. What a difference cropping makes!

Try This!

It's a slow news day and your editor wants you — his star photojournalist — to take a photo for the front page. The best news photos tell a story. Explore your neighborhood and talk to people. What's on their minds?

Video Games & the Net

Video games use lots of catchy music, sound effects and, yes, even violence to hook players. And it works.

Games may be created by companies like Mad Loon Games, which work under contract to a publisher, or publishers may make games themselves. Creating a game requires dozens of talented workers, millions of dollars and can take from one to three years to produce. (Including lots of late nights!)

In turn, game publishers manufacture, package and market the game. They take a big risk when they release a new product. There are lots of other games out there, and competition is stiff. Only a few games become big sellers. In exchange for taking the risk, publishers take most of the profits.

And there are big profits in the video game business. Nintendo has sold more than 40 million copies of *Super Mario Brothers* around the world. (Mario sure has been busy! He's appeared in twenty-six games that have sold more than 152 million copies in total.)

Game designer Max McLoon creates the game and works with the team to design how it will play.

Artist Wanda B. Warhol creates the look of everything that will appear onscreen.

Animator Moe Shun uses computer software to make the characters' movements look real.

The Fine Print: Don't forget to apply the Big Six (see page 5) to the games you play!

55

Video Game Shame!

No kidding, Max! Entering the video game universe can be a little strange. Although manufacturers try to make their games as realistic as possible, stereotyped characters sometimes creep in. Researchers have found that most of the characters — and nearly all game heroes — are white. Blacks and Hispanics usually appear only as athletes. Even more worrying, when animals like Max appear in games, they're usually targets. Yikes!

And where are the women? A lot of games don't have many female characters. And when women do appear, they're usually dressed in revealing clothes that show off their (ahem) assets.

Then there's all that blood and gore. Some experts believe that violent video games encourage violence in the real world. Many bestselling games, for example, reward players for killing. And few games ever show the effects of violence on victims. Even games rated "E" for "everyone" often contain violence. Would you let your younger sister or brother play violent video games? Why or why not?

WORST JOBS IN VIDEO GAMES

- *Gran Turismo* crossing guard
- *World Series Baseball* sports agent
- *Super Mario* barber
- *Pokémon* janitor
- *Quake* hostage
- *Grand Theft Auto* parking lot attendant
- *Tony Hawk Pro Skater* safety inspector
- *Tetris* block dropper

High Score Marketing

While you're concentrating on getting the high score, advertisers are concentrating on getting their messages to you. Some games feature product placement — company logos and actual products appear in the games. Gaming companies believe the products make the game more realistic, and manufacturers think placement enhances their product's image.

There are also "advergames" — free Internet-based games usually found on corporate Web sites that feature actual products. One car manufacturer, for instance, had a driving game in which players could choose a car and take it for a virtual spin. (No word on whether any virtual speeding tickets were handed out.)

Try This!

Next time you're gaming, look for a stereotyped character. What would happen if the character's race, gender or skills were altered? For example, a standard muscular warrior might become a muscular female warrior. Feeling creative? Break out the colored pencils and draw your new and improved video game character.

9090999
SCORE

Web Surfing

Back	Forward	Refresh	Home	AutoFill	Print	Mail	Stop

http://www.maxmcloon.com

Slurp!

Gross Out Soda!
Order a case today!
Only **$399.99**

maxmcloon.com HOME MUSIC GAMES CHAT CONTESTS SHOP

LOG IN   SEARCH [   ] GO

Today on maxmcloon.com

Adventurer Max McLoon Discovers Bigfoot!

World-famous adventurer Max McLoon has discovered proof that Bigfoot exists. Read about his amazing discovery in this exclusive interview! Full story ...

Max McLoon Inaction Figure!

Only **$899.99**

Beak rings below cost!!!

Just **$799.99**

■ Annoying pop-up ad

Exclusive offer! Subscribe to COOL LOON and save $$$$!

Just click on this pop-up ad and give us a credit card number — any credit card number will do, as long as we can charge it!

U mmm, "neat" Web site, Max …
The Internet certainly is an amazing tool. You already know the Net is a vast system of linked computer networks that lets you download photos, transfer files, post blogs and e-mail and instant message (IM). It's fun to research homework, get the latest news and info, join chat rooms and (of course) shop — without getting out of your pajamas!

But there are drawbacks. While there's lots of great info on the Net, there's also lots of junk. And sometimes it's difficult to separate facts from opinions online. Some official-looking Web sites fool readers into thinking they're getting fair information when they're not. Other Web sites are just plain sloppy — they have "facts" that aren't true at all. There are even fake Web sites with totally made-up stories.

You know you're spending too much time online when your best friend is the tech support guy at your Internet provider!

WEB CHECK!

Here are some ways to tell if a Web site is reliable:
- Look for sites created by credible sources such as museums, universities, governments and well-known media.
- Double-check info you find online with trusted books, magazines, knowledgeable people or other Web sites.
- Visit the site's "About Us" or "Who We Are" sections to check on the background of its creators. Are they qualified to write about the subject?
- Check to see when the page was last updated. Information on the Net can quickly become outdated — especially gossip about celebrities!
- Don't forget common sense — if something seems too good to be true, it probably is.

Try This!

Become a Web critic! Apply the Big Six (see page 5) to the Web sites you visit, and let your friends know when you've come across a great site — or a lousy one. Explain why you like or dislike it. Who sponsors the site? Is it used to promote a product or share experiences and opinions? Is it easy or hard to use? How does it compare to similar sites? (Checking out sites that are good, bad and ugly will give you ideas if you ever design your own.)

Mouse Click Marketing

O nce upon a time, the Internet had no advertising. Really! But as more people went online, advertisers quickly followed. Now it's hard to get away from uninvited e-mail ads, called "spam." Most e-mail ads have a clear message: send money now!

But online marketing doesn't stop at e-mail. It also includes Web sites. While personal Web sites are created by ordinary people to share info about hobbies, commercial Web sites are produced by companies who want to promote their products.

Corporate Web sites are usually super slick and use colorful graphics, animation and cool images to attract your attention. Some also offer exciting games or contests where you can win products, join chat rooms or download goodies such as funky screen savers that turn your computer screen into ads. All of these features keep users coming back.

HERBAL SMART PILLS

ENLARGER BEAK

Argh! All I did was register at a Web site to play a video game!

Little Web Lies

Sometimes Web sites ask you to provide your name, e-mail address and other personal information to access their news, software and services. (Some sites also tempt you to hand over personal info through surveys, contests, games and clubs.)

This information helps the site's creators learn more about its visitors. But be careful! Some sites may sell your personal information to online marketers, who'll use your e-mail address to send spam.

Many sites also send small files called "cookies" to your computer. These cookies let the site "remember" information about you, such as preferences and passwords. But cookies can also be used to track your activity on a Web site, letting its administrators collect information about your interests and habits. Creepy!

There are easy ways to protect your privacy from unwanted online intruders. To avoid spam, get a separate e-mail account for Web sites and people you don't know that well. Keep your main e-mail address just for friends and family.

I get creative when registering for a site. How do they know my real name isn't I.P. Alott?

WORLD WIDE WEIRDOS

Beware of weirdos when you're exploring the online world. Since you can't see people, you can't be sure if your new cyber pal is an eleven-year-old girl or a forty-year-old ex-con.

To protect yourself, avoid revealing personal information, such as your real name, address, phone number, school name or passwords, to online strangers. Sounds obvious, right? But it's amazing how many people let complete strangers know all about their personal lives.

If you encounter anything or anyone creepy — even someone who seems nice but wants to get personal — tell your parents immediately.

Visit your favorite search engine and type in "Internet safety tips." You'll find more good ideas for protecting yourself online. Who wants to be a victim?

Shh! Internet Secret!

Some companies pay people to visit chat rooms and online forums and promote their products to unsuspecting Web surfers.

Fast Forward

Media change all the time. (Even TV was once considered new.) No one's really sure what kind of crazy media we'll be reading, watching and listening to in the future. But one thing is sure — you can ask the Big Six (on page 5) of all the messages you're exposed to, now and even in 2050!

It's 2050. Dominic and Michael may look older, but check out the new technology.

1. Booming speakers woven into the fabric of this SoundBlaster Suit let you feel your favorite music all day long. (Not recommended for the ticklish.)
2. Create animated holographic sculptures and e-mail them to your pals with VirtuaGloves!
3. CommCenter automatically blocks vid-marketers and alters your appearance so you always look your best for video calls.
4. Stylish and multi-functional All Media Suit features holographic keyboard, finger-camera, chest-mounted photo printer and built-in video game controllers. (Also available in tweed.)
5. Eat a healthy balanced meal while catching up on your favorite shows with the TV Dinner TV!
6. No looking for this remote control — the ZapSpyder finds you!

Glossary

Advertising/commercials: Paid messages about products or services that are used to attract potential customers. Most media make their money by charging companies who want to advertise their products to the media's audience.

Advertorials: Newspaper and magazine articles that look like genuine editorial content but are actually paid messages sponsored by advertisers.

Bias: Favoring one side over another. Critics often accuse journalists of bias.

Brand loyalty: A consumer's loyalty to one brand over similar ones. For example, Max always buys Waste-O-Dough™ beak rings instead of Diss-Figeur™ beak rings.

Circulation: The number of copies distributed by a newspaper or magazine. The more copies a publication circulates, the more it can charge for advertising.

Crossover: A song that becomes popular with more than one type of audience. Max would have a crossover hit if his Country and Western CD became popular with hip-hopheads.

Facts: Information that's known to be true. (See Opinion)

Format: The content and style of a radio station designed to reach a specific audience. Top Forty and Country are two examples.

Genres: Types of media that share the same features or conventions. For example, some TV genres are sitcoms, dramas and soap operas.

Hook: A catchy musical phrase that grabs listeners in the first thirty seconds.

Jolts per minute (JPMs): Attention-getting devices, such as sound effects or quick camera edits, that jolt viewers and keep them glued to the television.

Licensing: A business arrangement in which the owner of a property (such as a character like Max) gives a manufacturer permission to make products based on the property in return for money. For example, a movie based on a comic book is licensing in action.

Medium/media: A medium is a method of communication. More than one medium is "media." The following media are examined in this book: television, radio, magazines, comic books, newspapers, video games and the Internet.

Network: A group of broadcasting stations that air the same programs. For example, American networks include ABC, NBC and CBS.

Opinion: A personal belief that is open to debate. (See Facts)

Playlists: Lists of videos or songs played on the radio or music video channels.

Ratings: Lists that show the popularity of radio and TV shows. The higher the ratings, the more money broadcasters can charge advertisers.

Spam: Unwanted e-mails from advertisers.

Stereotypes: Characters or groups that are oversimplified based on certain standard, but often untrue, characteristics — for example, dumb athletes.

Index